Countdown to Christmas:

Unwrap the Christmas Story with Your Family in 15 Days

Lisa Appelo
© November, 2015, 2017

Requests for information should be directed to:
lisa.appelo@gmail.com.

ISBN: 9780692990681

Cover Photo: JackyBrown (BigStock)
Cover Design: Five J's Design

To Ben, Rachel, Nick, Seth, Zach, Matt & Annalise

For all the days we opened God's Word and learned of Him together. You are incredible, each of you. And I love you fierce.

Table of Contents

Introduction

This nativity advent devotional grew out of my own desire to be more intentional with my children about the reason for Christmas. I've always loved nativity scenes. I've collected them over the years and during the Christmas season, we display them throughout our home on the mantel, on coffee tables, in the front yard and as ornaments on the tree.

I always have one kid-friendly manger scene that is completely accessible to my kids. They can play with it, rearrange it throughout the season and use it to re-enact the Christmas story. In the past, we've used a hand-made wooden set as well as a Playmobil® manger set (super popular with my boys) and a pretty but child-friendly resin set.

Last year, I put together a 15-day nativity activity, matching each of the standard pieces in a nativity scene with a portion of scripture, to unfold the story of Christ's birth. I knew our busy December would make a month-long study impractical. We'd surely miss days, then fall behind and then might drop it altogether.

But 15 days works for us. It gives us plenty of margin during the month and accommodates days when I know we'll be out of the house. Rather than adding one more must-do to our December list, I wanted to be able to carve out some time with my family, open this devotional book and focus on the birth of Jesus as we built one piece of our manger scene together each day for 15 days.

How to Use this Nativity Advent Devotional

Each day has a scripture, devotional reading, prayer and the instructions to add one piece from a standard nativity set. I've also included a suggested Christmas carol that ties in with that day's scripture. While the daily verse is included here, you may want to use your own Bible or have your children read from their Bibles.

You can start this countdown 15 days before Christmas or begin early in December, using the days that are convenient for your family. Each day, after reading the day's scripture and devotional, add the corresponding piece of the nativity to your manger scene. Your manger scene will fill out each day as you draw closer to Christmas Day. Close with your own prayer or the written prayer that's included and the suggested Christmas carol.

I pray this becomes a beautiful tradition for your family and helps you set aside time to teach the meaning of Christmas as you make treasured memories with your children.

Merry Christmas as we celebrate our Savior!

Lisa Appelo

Day 1: The Crèche

Scripture: Micah 5:2

"But you, Bethlehem Ephrathah , though you are little among the thousands of Judah, Yet out of you shall come forth to Me The One to be Ruler in Israel, Whose goings forth are from of old, From everlasting [NKJV]."

Devotional Reading

Around 700 years before Jesus was ever born, a prophet named Micah foretold that Jesus would be born in Bethlehem. Seven hundred years is a long time! That would be like someone in the Middle Ages predicting the exact town where someone would be born today.

Bethlehem was a village about six miles from Jerusalem. It's in a very hilly part of Israel and you have to walk up steep hills to reach it. The name Bethlehem means "house of bread." This would be the house of bread alright. Of all the villages and all the towns and cities in the world, Jesus, who said he was the Bread of Life, would be born in Bethlehem.

In the key verse, we see the prophet Micah foretold something else very important about the One who would be born in Bethlehem. The verse says he would be "from of old, from everlasting." What do you think that means? How could a newborn baby be from "of old" or from everlasting?

He can't. Only God is from everlasting. God has always existed, before any of this world was ever created. (John 1:1-2) So Micah the prophet tells us not only that the Messiah would be born in Bethlehem, but that He is God Himself born as a baby.

Messiah is the Jewish word for Christ. The Jewish people were excited for the Messiah to come. Other prophets had also told them about the coming Messiah and they waited expectantly for hundreds and hundreds of years, knowing He would one day be born in Bethlehem.

Nativity Activity

Put up your stable or crèche today. Though we still have a few weeks before we celebrate Jesus' birthday, we wait eagerly, just as the people eagerly awaited the Messiah's birth. And just like you know where and when you'll celebrate Christmas, God knew where and when Jesus would be born.

Prayer

Dear God, thank You that You know all things and nothing is hidden from You. You have always been and will always be and You know what will happen tomorrow and the next day and the next. Nothing surprises You. And because of that, God, we trust Your timing, even when it feels like we're waiting. Help us to trust You when it's hard. Thank You, God, for being a promise keeper and for fulfilling every single promise You've made so perfectly. Amen.

Suggested Christmas Carol

Come Thou Long Expected Jesus

Day 2: The Palm Tree

Scripture: Isaiah 11:1-2

"A shoot will come up from the stump of Jesse; from his roots a Branch will bear fruit. The Spirit of the LORD will rest on him -- the Spirit of wisdom and of understanding, the Spirit of counsel and of might, the Spirit of the knowledge and fear of the LORD [NIV]."

Devotional Reading

Today we're talking about stumps and shoots. Do you have any stumps from old trees in your yard? Our yard is full of towering oak trees and every now and again, we have a tree surgeon come out to trim up dead branches and cut down any old, weak trees. Last year, one of our granddaddy oak trees was cut down to a stump. Do you know what happened a few weeks later? New green shoots started growing right out of that old stump.

That's the picture that the prophet Isaiah uses. Isaiah prophesied about 700 years before Jesus was ever born and foretold that a new shoot would come from Jesse. To understand

Isaiah's prophecy about stumps and shoots, we first need to know a little about Jesus' own family tree.

Jesus was descended from King David, the great king who reigned over Israel. In fact, both Mary and Joseph were in the line of King David. King David's father was named Jesse. For several hundreds of years, one of King David's royal descendants sat on the throne of Israel, and then Judah. But the last Davidic king was taken prisoner by the Babylonians and his sons were killed.

Israel then went through a series of foreign rulers like the Babylonians and Persians and Romans, and King David's royal line looked dead -- like an old, rotting stump.

But out of what looked like a dead royal line, God brought a new shoot. This shoot was the Messiah, Jesus, who would be a new king. He didn't rule like King David did. Jesus didn't have a palace or throne or royal robes on earth. Jesus' kingdom is a heavenly kingdom and He left all the glory of a king to come to earth as a baby.

Nativity Scene

Add a palm tree or plant to your nativity scene to represent the shoot that came from the stump of Jesse.

Prayer

Lord, nothing is too hard for You. You are able, even when things look impossible. You are able, even when hope looks dead. You are able, even when there seems to be no way. Every promise You make will be fulfilled, even when circumstances make it look improbable. Help us to believe this with our whole heart and help us to live fully trusting You. Amen.

Suggested Christmas Carol

Lo! How a Rose E'er Blooming

Day 3: The Cattle

Scripture: Isaiah 7:14

"Therefore the LORD Himself will give you a sign: The virgin will conceive and give birth to a son, and will call him Immanuel [NIV]."

Devotional Reading

Today's verse is another very specific prophecy written about 700 years before Jesus was born. One thing's for sure: the birth of Jesus wasn't a secret. For thousands of years, God had promised a Messiah. The Old Testament is full of signs and information that God revealed to people about the coming Messiah.

There are likely signs all around you that Christmas Day is coming. When you look around and see the Christmas trees and lights going up, hear Christmas music on the radio and begin to celebrate with Christmas parties and plays, it's exciting because you know December 25th is approaching. The Jews had a similar excitement as they waited and watched for signs that the Messiah had come.

One of the signs that God said He would give was extraordinary -- a virgin would become pregnant and would give birth to a baby boy. This could only happen through a miracle and only God could make this happen.

God also said the Messiah would be called Immanuel. What does Immanuel mean? Another verse in the Bible tells us that Immanuel means "God with us." [Matthew 1:23]

God with us. That's how it had been in the beginning. When God created Adam and Eve, God walked with them in the garden. God was with Adam and Eve and talked with them. But then Adam and Eve disobeyed God, choosing to do the one thing God had told them not to do. And from that time on, everything changed. Because of their sin, Adam and Eve could no longer be with God. Sin keeps us from His holiness.

So, when God announced that the coming Messiah would be called Immanuel, it meant God would again be *with us*. God the Son would walk with people, live with them, eat with them, celebrate with them, teach them, disciple them, heal them. You bet the Jewish people were excited about the coming Messiah! Jesus would be *Immanuel -- God with us.*

Nativity Activity

Add the cattle to your nativity scene. Can you imagine the mess and odor of the cattle next to baby Jesus, *God with us,* who is very God of very God? He left the perfection of heaven to come down and be with us, in our simple, ordinary, grubby lives.

Prayer

Dear Lord, what a miracle You have done. Thank You that You are a *with-us* God. Thank You for coming down to us – for piercing time and space to appear to us where we are. You pursued us when we least deserved it. Thank You, Lord, that even today, You do not stay far off but walk with us in our struggles and joy; in our work and our worries; and in our disappointments and celebrations. Help us know Your presence. We love You and we praise You for being a with-us God. Amen.

Suggested Christmas Carol

O Come, O Come Emmanuel

Day 4: Mary

Scripture: Luke 1:26-33

"In the sixth month of Elizabeth's pregnancy, God sent the angel Gabriel to Nazareth, a town in Galilee, to a virgin pledged to be married to a man named Joseph, a descendant of David. The virgin's name was Mary. The angel went to her and said, 'Greetings, you who are highly favored! The Lord is with you.' Mary was greatly troubled at his words and wondered what kind of greeting this might be. But the angel said to her, 'Do not be afraid, Mary; you have found favor with God. You will conceive and give birth to a son, and you are to call him Jesus. He will be great and will be called the Son of the Most High. The Lord God will give him the throne of his father, David, and he will reign over Jacob's descendants forever; his kingdom will never end [NIV].'"

Devotional Reading

Mary was a young, Jewish girl living in a small, rural village. The Bible doesn't tell us exactly how old Mary was, but most Jewish girls in that time period got engaged and married much younger than girls today. Mary was probably a teenager – somewhere between 13 and 16 years old. She probably did things typical of girls her age – helping to cook for her family, going to market for household needs, maybe helping to mend or make new clothes for the family.

We don't know much about her family, which means they were probably an ordinary Jewish family making life in an ordinary, rural village. But right in the midst of that ordinary came an extraordinary announcement. The angel Gabriel appeared to Mary with startling news.

Mary might have been frightened but the angel assured her that God highly favored her and that He was with her. God's favor meant that God would grace Mary with a special blessing.

Then Gabriel announced that, although Mary was a virgin, she would be with child and would give birth to a son. And Gabriel told her exactly what to name this son -- Jesus. That's how Jesus got His name! God named Him! Tomorrow we'll find out why He is named Jesus.

Gabriel also told Mary that Jesus would be the Son of God. He would be a king and would rule forever with a kingdom that would never end. Remember that Jesus was in the royal line of King David? Now there could be no doubt. This was the promised Messiah. It all fit. The Messiah was the Son of God, born of a virgin, who would not usher in an earthly kingdom, but a heavenly kingdom without end.

A young, Jewish girl told she would deliver the Messiah. *The Son of God.* Yes, God had graced Mary with the highest blessing.

Nativity Activity

Place the figure of Mary in your nativity scene. Mary wasn't in Bethlehem when the angel made his announcement; she was still many miles away in her small hometown of Nazareth. But we'll put the figure of Mary in the nativity today to remind us that she was the first one Gabriel told about baby Jesus.

Prayer

Lord, help us to be humble as Your servant, Mary, was humble. Unlike this world that favors the loudest and the strongest,

19

help us to remember that You favor the humble. Thank You, Father, for using our ordinary lives to do extraordinary kingdom work. Help us to obey whatever path You have for us and wherever You lead us. May Your glory shine brightly through us as we offer You our simple and ordinary lives.

Suggested Christmas Carol

Mary, Did You Know?

Day 5: Joseph

Scripture: Matthew 1:18-21

"Now the birth of Jesus was as follows: After His mother Mary was betrothed to Joseph, before they came together, she was found with child of the Holy Spirit. Then Joseph her husband, being a just man, and not wanting to make her a public example, was minded to put her away secretly. But while he thought about these things, behold, an angel of the Lord appeared to him in a dream, saying, 'Joseph, son of David, do not be afraid to take to you Mary your wife, for that which is conceived in her is of the Holy Spirit. And she will bring forth a Son, and you shall call His name JESUS, for He will save His people from their sins [NKJV].'"

Devotional Reading

Joseph was a carpenter who also lived in the small town of Nazareth, where Mary lived. Joseph and Mary were engaged and like other engaged couples of that day, it's likely they barely knew each other and would not have spent time alone together.

21

And yet, one day, Joseph learned some startling news: Mary was expecting a baby. We don't know exactly how Joseph learned this information. Maybe he heard the news in town one afternoon. Or perhaps a relative or customer in his woodshop relayed the news to him.

The Bible does make this clear: Joseph was a just man -- he did what was right and fair. He didn't want Mary humiliated, so rather than make a public spectacle, he'd decided to quietly divorce her. Engagements were so binding back then that a divorce decree was needed to break an engagement.

Well, God had other plans. He sent an angel to Joseph in a dream. The angel told him that Mary's pregnancy was the work of the Holy Spirit. She would have a son that Joseph was to name Jesus. Just exactly what the angel had told Mary! Good thing they couldn't argue over the name.

Then the angel delivered the most amazing news: this baby, Jesus, would save His people from their sins. Jesus in Hebrew is Yeshua [yeh SHOO a]. It means the LORD (Yahweh) saves.

How would Jesus save people from their sin? Sin is something we think, say or do that is disobedient to God. The Bible says the punishment for sin is death. Because of our sin – and we've all done it – we would be forever separated from God in death.

But Jesus paid the punishment for us. [1 John 2:2] Because Jesus never sinned, when He died on a cross, He became a substitute, taking the punishment for our sin. After Jesus was buried, He rose on the third day to eternal life, giving everyone who believes in Him as Savior eternal life also.

Payment for sin and the promise of eternal life. The long-awaited Redeemer who would save people from their sins would soon be born.

Nativity Activity

Add the figure of Joseph to your nativity scene. Joseph obeyed God and was kind and fair to Mary as they prepared for the birth of Jesus.

Prayer

Dear Lord, we confess to You that we have sinned. We have done things and said things and thought things that are wrong and though You have always loved us, we have sinned against You. Thank You that You forgive. Thank You that Jesus saves us from our sins. Thank You for sending Your son to die on a cross to pay the punishment for my sin. I accept the free gift of grace and eternal life that You give because of Jesus' death and I want to live out my life obeying You and bringing You glory. Amen.

Suggested Christmas Carol

Silent Night, Holy Night

Day 6: The Donkey

Scripture: Luke 2:1-5

"And it came to pass in those days that a decree went out from Caesar Augustus that all the world should be registered. This census first took place while Quirinius was governing Syria. So all went to be registered, everyone to his own city. Joseph also went up from Galilee, out of the city of Nazareth, into Judea, to the city of David, which is called Bethlehem, because he was of the house and lineage of David, to be registered with Mary, his betrothed wife, who was with child [NKJV]."

Devotional Reading

Have you ever packed up and gone on a long trip? You probably traveled in a car or on a plane. Can you imagine walking to get where you needed to go?

Joseph and Mary would have walked for many days to get from Nazareth to Bethlehem. Many pictures show Mary riding on a donkey but scripture doesn't tell us that. It is possible that Mary rode on a donkey, though, since she was pregnant.

As they walked the dusty roads to Bethlehem, I wonder if they were worried? Had they left behind a special cradle lovingly built by Joseph the carpenter? Did they look up at the stars as they camped in the evenings and wonder how God would take care of them so far from home? Did they know that this unexpected journey just when Mary was about to have a baby was precisely where God wanted them?

God knew exactly how He would take care of them. It wasn't an inconvenient Roman edict that brought Mary and Joseph to Bethlehem. God Himself had planned every bit of this story. Remember when we learned that Mary and Joseph were descended from the royal line of King David?

King David's father was Jesse, and Jesse's father was Obed and Obed's father was Boaz. Boaz and Ruth had lived in Bethlehem, so when Caesar Augustus ordered everyone to be registered for a census, Joseph and Mary had to go back to the village of their ancestors to be counted. And where were their ancestors from? Bethlehem. Just like the old prophet Micah had foretold 700 years earlier.

Things were working out exactly as God had planned.

Nativity Activity

Add the donkey to the nativity scene. While we don't know for certain that Mary rode a donkey, the donkey represents the long journey that Joseph and Mary took to arrive in Bethlehem.

Prayer

Dear Lord, there are times when our circumstances aren't going well, when it seems like things aren't working out and it doesn't feel like You are in charge. But we are reminded, today, that You rule over everything – even over governments and inconvenience and where we are born. Help us to trust You and Your purposes when we cannot see what You are up to. Help us to know that You lead us with purpose and precision and that You always, always deal with us in love. In Jesus' name, Amen.

Suggest Christmas Carol

O Little Town of Bethlehem

Day 7: The Manger

Scripture: Luke 2:12

"And this will be the sign to you: You will find a Babe wrapped in swaddling cloths, lying in a manger [NKJV]."

Devotional Reading

Kings are usually born in palaces. Imagine the kinds of castles and palaces where kings are born. There are large rooms filled with exquisite tapestries and opulent furnishings. Gilded mirrors and fine oil paintings decorate the walls while jeweled and silver boxes line the dressing table. The crib is draped with luxurious bedding in royal colors and the best of attendants are there to meet every possible need. The birth of a new king is usually accompanied with the extravagant pomp of full nobility.

The birth of King Jesus was completely different. After the long trip from Nazareth, Joseph and Mary arrived in the small village of Bethlehem. This little village was bustling with travelers from all over Israel who had come to register for the census.

Because of the crowds, the inn was completely filled. There was no vacancy anywhere in the village.

And so this young couple, weary after their dusty journey, found the only comfortable shelter they could -- in a barn or a cave that served as a stable for animals. The time was getting close for Jesus to be born. But here? In a stable? Such a humble place for a king to be born.

No fancy crib draped with royal bedding here. There was only the crib used as a feeding trough for the cows and donkeys. This humble wooden manger -- probably lined with handfuls of fresh, sweet hay -- would be the first earthly bed for the King of Kings and Lord of Lords.

Nativity Activity

Place the manger in your nativity scene. Mary and Joseph must have been getting excited, because they knew that any day, Jesus would be born.

Prayer

Dear Jesus, we are in awe that You would leave the riches of heaven and become poor for our sakes. We are in awe that You

29

would leave the glory of heaven and walk in humbleness for us. You teach us that our life is not to be about wealth or position or comfort. Lord we ask You to meet our needs as You have promised; we ask that You keep us from loving riches above You; and we ask that You would help us to steward well all that You allow to come through our hand. Amen.

Suggested Christmas Carol

Away in a Manger

Day 8: Baby Jesus

Scripture: Luke 2:6-7

"So it was, that while they were there, the days were completed for her to be delivered. And she brought forth her firstborn Son, and wrapped Him in swaddling cloths, and laid Him in a manger, because there was no room for them in the inn [NKJV]."

Devotional Reading

Oh happy day! It had been months since the angel first announced that Mary would be pregnant and would give birth to a son. Mary had been so excited, so humbled, so overwhelmed at God's goodness. To think that she would be the mother of the long-awaited Messiah!

God had done just as He had promised and Mary had delivered a healthy baby boy. Before the world was ever created, God had ordained this exact moment, in this exact town, with these exact parents for the birth of Jesus. For thousands of years, the prophets and followers of God had longed to see this day.

Think about how stunning it must have been -- to swaddle the Son of God as a newborn. The holy, majestic, all-powerful, all-knowing God of the universe took on dimpled skin and downy hair. God the Son pierced time and space. The same God who spoke all creation into being; the same God who flooded the earth while safeguarding Noah and his family; the same God who shook Mt. Sinai with thunder and lightning as He gave the 10 commandments took on the vulnerable flesh of an infant.

How tiny He was! How soft His cries and how delicate His fist that curled around Joseph's calloused finger. Mary wrapped Him tenderly in the swaddling clothes they had brought with them and laid Him gently on the soft hay of the manger.

As they watched their baby boy sleep, Joseph and Mary must have thought back to all that the angel had told them. *This was the Son of the Most High. He would be great. He would save His people from their sins. His kingdom would never end.*

Oh, it was so much to take in. Tonight, they would simply thank God for their healthy, new baby and for the miracle of the Messiah in their midst.

Nativity Activity

Place baby Jesus in the manger of your nativity scene. The birth of Jesus might have been quiet that night, but it changed the world forever. What a glorious night!

Prayer

Tonight, God, we praise You. We praise You for Your majesty and glory, for being Creator and sustainer. We praise You for Your goodness, love, mercy, kindness, compassion, patience, justice. We praise You for being the First and the Last, the Alpha and Omega, the Beginning and the End. We magnify You. Your glory fills the whole earth. May our home and our hearts be filled to the full with You this Christmas and long after. Amen.

Suggested Christmas Carol

O Holy Night

Day 9: The Shepherd

Scripture: Luke 2:8-11

"Now there were in the same country shepherds living out in the fields, keeping watch over their flocks by night. And behold, an angel of the Lord stood before them, and the glory of the Lord shone around them, and they were greatly afraid. Then the angel said to them, 'Do not be afraid, for behold, I bring you good tidings of great joy which will be to all people For there is born to you this day in the city of David a Savior, who is Christ the Lord [NKJV].'"

Devotional Reading

When Jesus was born, no church bells started ringing. No Christmas lights or Christmas carols heralded the birth of Jesus. Most people in Bethlehem kept right on with their business, completely unaware that the Messiah had been born in their midst.

But God did send one birth announcement that night -- to a group of shepherds camping outdoors and watching over their flocks on fields outside of Bethlehem. Now shepherds weren't the most important or the most distinguished or the wealthiest people of that area. In fact, the shepherds were pretty low and despised on the Hebrew social scale. God could have chosen to announce Jesus' birth to someone much more important – like the Jewish High Priest or the rich merchants in Jerusalem or even the Roman governor.

Instead, God chose to send His angel to plain and simple shepherds. Imagine their shock when the pitch-black night sky was suddenly lit up by the glory of the Lord! They were terrified! They had seen plenty of bears and wolves and lions while guarding their sheep, but never had an angel appeared on their night watch.

"Do not be afraid," the angel assured them. And then the angel announced good news of great joy which would be for all people. All nations on earth, people from every country, every continent, every tribe and every language would benefit from this good news. That very day, a Savior, Christ the Lord, had been born right there in Bethlehem.

The shepherds must have looked at the angel with wonder. Could it be? The Messiah, the One their people had spoken of, read about, prayed for, and longed for had now been born? Oh, this *was* good news! I bet their hearts beat a little quicker, they broke into smiles and clapped each other on the back. Messiah had come! This was *very* good news.

Nativity Activity

Add the shepherd to your nativity scene in celebration of the good news of Jesus' birth that the angel announced to the shepherds. We'll learn more about them in a couple of days.

Prayer

Dear God, thank You that Christmas is good news for all people. Thank You that Your good news is for the rich and poor, the old and young, the parent and child, who live in any country and who speak any language. Thank You that You came for the lowly as much as those with power. Help us, Lord, to care about others as You do, regardless of whether we live in the same neighborhood or the same country. In Jesus' name, Amen.

Suggested Christmas Carol

While Shepherds Watched Their Flocks By Night

Day 10: The Angel

Scripture: Luke 2:13-14

"Suddenly a great company of the heavenly host appeared with the angel, praising God and saying: 'Glory to God in the highest heaven, and on earth peace to those on whom his favor rests [NIV].'"

Devotional Reading

Yesterday, we read that one angel appeared to a group of shepherds on the night that Jesus was born. Do you remember how terrified the shepherds were? Well, right after the angel announced Jesus' birth, an entire army of angels joined in and filled the night sky.

The Bible doesn't tell us how many angels there were but describes it as a multitude. Revelation 5 gives us a hint that there were more angels than the shepherds could possibly have counted. Revelation 5:11 says that the number of angels around God's throne is "ten thousand times ten thousand, and thousands of thousands."

If you multiply 10,000 times 10,000, that is 100 million angels! That's way more than 1,000 or 100 thousands or even a million. That is 100 millions. That's the number of angels around God's throne and God sent a multitude of them to the shepherds.

Well, this quiet night had sure changed into a huge celebration! What were these angels doing? They were praising God! Imagine the dark night sky lit up by more angels than the shepherds could possibly count all saying, "Glory to God in heaven! Glory to God in heaven!"

The angels also proclaimed peace. This didn't mean a world peace where there would never again be war or fighting or arguments. The angels were proclaiming peace between God and man. Remember when we talked about our problem of sin a few days ago? When we sin, we become God's enemy because we choose to disobey God and rebel against Him.

But when Jesus was born and then died on the cross to pay the punishment for our sin, He made peace between God and man. When we believe that Jesus died for our sin, we can ask God to forgive us and through Jesus we can have peace with God. This is salvation peace and it means that we are no longer an enemy of

God. Instead, we become God's friend and we have all of the blessings of God.

Nativity Activity

Add the angel to your nativity scene today. When you look at this angel, you can try to imagine the thousands or millions of angels that appeared to the shepherds and praised God the night that Jesus was born!

Prayer

Dear God, thank You that the birth of Your Son, Jesus, makes peace between God and men possible. Thank You for forgiving us and that we can be a follower as well as Your friend. We do not take that lightly, Lord, but accept it as a great gift and a blessing that flows only because of Jesus. We love You, Lord. Amen.

Suggested Christmas Carol

Hark! The Herald Angels Sing

Day 11: The Sheep

Scripture: Luke 2:15-18

"So it was when the angels had gone away from them into heaven, that the shepherds said to one another, 'Let us now go to Bethlehem and see this thing that has come to pass, which the Lord has made known to us.' And they came with haste and found Mary and Joseph, and the Babe lying in a manger. Now when they had seen Him, they made widely known the saying which was told them concerning this Child. And all those who heard it marveled at those things which were told them by the shepherds [NKJV]."

Devotional Reading

It wasn't enough for the shepherds to simply hear the good news that Jesus had been born. They wanted to see Jesus for themselves. They didn't wait around for a day off or even wait until morning.

As soon as the multitude of angels went back to heaven, the shepherds hurried from those dark, dew-covered fields into

Bethlehem to find the baby Jesus. I wonder if they left anyone in charge of their sheep? I bet they didn't take the sheep with them because herding their sheep into Bethlehem would have been a slow and cumbersome process and today's verses say the shepherds came with haste.

The shepherds were probably in fields only a few miles away from Bethlehem. Once in Bethlehem, the shepherds searched for baby Jesus. The angel had told them that Jesus was in a manger, but the angel hadn't told them exactly which stable. But sure enough: the shepherds found baby Jesus just as the angel had said – lying in a manger next to Mary and Joseph.

How do you think the shepherds approached Jesus? Do you think they kneeled to honor Him? Or do you think they began praising God as they had seen the angels do earlier? We don't know what the shepherds said or did when they saw Jesus, but this night would forever impact them.

Because after seeing Jesus, they told people everywhere the good news that the Savior, the Messiah and Lord, had been born. You see, it wasn't enough just to hear the angel's good news that Jesus had been born. And it wasn't enough to see Jesus for themselves. They wanted others to know. The shepherds shared the amazing news that Jesus had been born with everyone they met.

Nativity Activity

Place the sheep in your nativity scene. The shepherds were the first people in the whole world besides Joseph and Mary to see Jesus the night he was born. And they were the first people in the whole world to share the good news of Jesus' birth with others.

Prayer

Dear God, with all of the busyness of parties and shopping this month, help us not to lose sight of the good news that a Savior has been born to us. Help us to be more excited about Jesus than anything else that happens this Christmas. And may we be so filled with the good news of Jesus that we want to share about Him with others as well. Amen.

Suggested Christmas Carol

Go Tell It on the Mountain

Day 12: The Star

Scripture: Matthew 2:1-2

"Now after Jesus was born in Bethlehem of Judea in the days of Herod the king, behold, wise men from the East came to Jerusalem, saying, 'Where is He who has been born King of the Jews? For we have seen His star in the East and have come to worship Him [NKJV].'"

Devotional Reading

Have you ever been out on a really clear night and looked up at the stars? How many did you see? In most cities and towns these days, we can only see the brightest stars. The city lights prevent us from seeing all the stars. But if you go somewhere with no street lights or porch lights or business lights, it is inky black and you can make out hundreds and hundreds of stars in the sky.

That's how it was in ancient times. The stars were clearly visible at night. People used the stars to help them navigate and travel from place to place and to learn about the seasons.

After Jesus was born, wise men from the East noticed a special star. God had caused a supernatural, stellar event in the night sky. People often call this the Star of Bethlehem. This star was spectacular and unusual, and these wise men who studied the stars knew what it meant: that Jesus the Messiah had been born.

Having seen the star, the wise men packed up and traveled to Jerusalem to find Jesus. It would have taken them many weeks and maybe even months to travel all the way to Jerusalem. I imagine these wise men traveled with quite a caravan of camels, pack animals, food, water, tents, blankets and special gifts for Jesus.

When they arrived in Jerusalem, they went to King Herod and asked him where they could find Jesus. "We...have come to worship Him," they said. You see, the wise men didn't make the long journey to Jerusalem because they were curious about a star. They made the trip because they wanted to worship Jesus.

Nativity Activity

Who were these wise men and how did they know so much about Jesus? We'll learn more tomorrow but for today, place the star on your nativity scene. If your nativity set doesn't have a star, you can make one with paper and attach it to the top of the stable.

Prayer

Dear God, these wise men remind us that Christmas is a time to worship Jesus. We worship You for being almighty and all wise. We worship You for being Creator and Redeemer. We worship You for being Savior and Sustainer. You are the only one worthy of our worship. And so today, we give You glory and honor. Amen.

Suggested Christmas Carol

The First Noel

Day 13: First Wise Man

Scripture: Matthew 2:3-5; 7-8

"When Herod the king heard this, he was troubled, and all Jerusalem with him. And when he had gathered all the chief priests and scribes of the people together, he inquired of them where the Christ was to be born. So they said to him, 'In Bethlehem of Judea' ... Then Herod, when he had secretly called the wise men, determined from them what time the star appeared. And he sent them to Bethlehem and said, 'Go and search carefully for the young Child, and when you have found Him, bring back word to me, that I may come and worship Him also [NKJV].'"

Devotional Reading

Today, let's look at who these wise men were and how they knew so much about Jesus. Yesterday, we learned they were from the East. The wise men are also called magi. The magi were originally from Persia. If you look on a globe, Persia was located where Iraq is today.

The magi studied the planets, stars, and other heavenly bodies and events to advise kings. The magi were not kings themselves, though they usually held very high positions in the royal court and were often very wealthy.

The magi also weren't Jewish. So how did the magi know so much about Jesus? Well, long before Jesus was born, many Jews had been exiled to Persia. Both Daniel (of lion's den fame) and Esther (of Queen Esther fame) were Jews who had lived in Persia. Even after the exile, many Jews stayed in the Persian empire.

The magi of Persia probably learned about God and the promise of a Messiah from the Jews who lived in Persia. Since the magi were highly educated, they would have studied the Old Testament, including the prophecies about a coming Messiah. The magi would have passed down this knowledge to succeeding generations of magi.

So when these wise men from the East saw the spectacular and unusual Star of Bethlehem, they recognized it as a sign that the long-awaited Jesus the Messiah had been born. They would journey many miles and many weeks to search for Jesus.

Nativity Activity

Add the first wise man to your nativity scene. While, traditionally, most nativity scenes include three wise men, the Bible doesn't say how many there were. There were at least two, but there could have been five or seven or 12. Today, just set up the first wise man. We have more to explore tomorrow.

Prayer

Dear Lord, You tell us that if we ask, it will be given; if we seek, we will find; and if we knock, the door will be opened. Thank You that You are not hidden from us but that we can know You. Every day as we read about Jesus' birth we are seeking You and we want to find You in scripture. Help us to keep seeking You even after all the presents are opened and the decorations are put away. In Jesus' name, Amen.

Suggested Christmas Carol

What Child Is This?

Day 14: Second Wise Man

Scripture: Matthew 2:9-11a

"When [the wise men] heard the king, they departed; and behold, the star which they had seen in the East went before them, till it came and stood over where the young Child was. When they saw the star, they rejoiced with exceedingly great joy. And when they had come into the house, they saw the young Child with Mary His mother, and fell down and worshipped Him [NKJV]."

Devotional Reading

This was no ordinary star. God caused this star to proceed before the wise men and lead them right to Bethlehem. In fact, this star stood still over the very house where young Jesus was. The wise men followed the star from Jerusalem to Bethlehem. What an adventure! They were filled to the full with joy and excitement! They had left their home in the East and had traveled for weeks or months hoping to find Jesus. And now, the amazing star had led these wise men straight to Him.

Two things had changed since the shepherds had visited Jesus. First, Jesus and His family were no longer in a stable. Joseph, Mary and Jesus lived in a house when the wise men arrived. Second, Jesus was no longer a newborn baby. Jesus was now a child and while scripture doesn't say exactly how old Jesus was, he was probably younger than two years old when the wise men arrived.

When the wise men saw Jesus, what did they do? They fell down and worshipped. Only God is worshipped. These wise men were not just book smart. They were spiritually smart. They understood and believed scripture and they knew that Jesus was the Messiah, God with us, and worthy of worship.

One more thing for today. Remember a few days ago, we read that the angel had said that the good news would be for all people? Remember we said that meant people of every country and language and tribe?

The wise men were from a different country and different language than the Jewish people. They were Gentiles. Already, the angel's announcement was coming true. These wise men had learned about the one true God and the coming Messiah and had committed to worshipping Jesus.

Nativity Activity

Add the second wise man to your nativity scene. Tomorrow, we'll look at one more important thing the wise men did when they found Jesus that is a key to our Christmas celebration.

Prayer

Today, we thank You, God, for the Bible. Thank You for the prophecies about Jesus' birth and for ensuring that the important events and information about Jesus' birth are recorded for us. Help us to be students of Your Word, as the wise men were students of the word they had. Open our eyes so that we are spiritually wise to know You and worship You. In Jesus' name, Amen.

Suggested Christmas Carol

O Come, All Ye Faithful

Day 15: Third Wise Man

Scripture: Matthew 2:11b

"And when [the wise men] had opened their treasures, they presented gifts to Him: gold, frankincense, and myrrh [NKJV]."

Devotional Reading

Christmas is all about presents! It's all about shopping and wrapping and opening up lots of presents, isn't that right? Wait. No? Then what is Christmas about?

Yes, it's about Jesus and celebrating the day He was born. Then why do we give presents to each other on Christmas?

The tradition of giving and exchanging presents started as a way to remember the gifts the wise men brought to Jesus. We don't know how many wise men came to see Jesus, but we do know that they brought three presents: gold, frankincense, and myrrh.

Gold is something you probably know about. Maybe your mom has a gold necklace or your dad has a gold watch. Gold is one of the most precious treasures on earth. It is used to create jewelry, coins, and other valuables.

You're probably less familiar with frankincense and myrrh. These were resins highly prized in ancient times. Frankincense was an expensive, fragrant incense and myrrh was a costly perfume.

These three gifts were fitting presents for Jesus. Gold was a customary present given to kings in ancient times and so it was the perfect present for King Jesus. Frankincense was burned as a fragrant offering to God which made it fitting as a present to Jesus, the Son of God. And myrrh was a perfume often used in burial. Why would a burial perfume be given to Jesus? Because Jesus came to earth to die on a cross and take away our sin. He was buried but He rose again to new life, just as He gives us new life.

So Christmas *is* about a present. But not the presents we give to each other. It's about the present that God gave *to us*. The most important, most precious gift ever given.

John 3:16 says, "For Go **so loved** the world, that **He gave** His one and only Son, that whosoever believes in Him, should not perish but have everlasting life." {emphasis added}

Jesus is the best gift of all.

Nativity Activity

Place the third Wise Man in your manger scene today. Go ahead and add in any other parts to your nativity set that we didn't talk about. We've learned the real reason we celebrate Christmas. It's not to give presents or to get more stuff. Christmas is the day we celebrate the best gift of all: the one that God gave to us in Jesus.

Prayer

Dear God, thank You giving us the best gift we could ever have. Thank You for Your Son, Jesus. Thank You for sending Him to be with us, to die on a cross and to bring us eternal life. Every gift under our tree and every gift we exchange helps us remember the best gift of Jesus. Help us to give presents and receive presents with joy because we celebrate Jesus. For from Him and through Him and for Him are all things. To Him be the glory forever! Amen.

Suggested Christmas Carol

Joy to the World! The Lord is Come

Countdown to Christmas

Your Family Memories

The space on these journaling pages has been created for you to record your family's advent memories. After reading through *Countdown to Christmas: Unwrap the Real Christmas Story with Your Family in 15 Days*, allow your children to respond to one or more of the following questions.

Older kids can record their own answers while younger children may want to dictate their answer to be written for them. Be sure to write the date to go back and remember years from now. The responses will become a cherished keepsake and remembrance of how your family prepared your hearts to celebrate Christmas.

Jesus is worth every bit of our celebration.

Questions

What part of the Christmas story did you learn this year?

What was the most special part of our Advent study this year?

What is your favorite piece of the nativity scene?

Why is Christmas special to you?

Why is Jesus special?

What gift do you want to give God this year?

Countdown to Christmas

_____

_____

_____

_____

_____

_____

_____

_____

_____

_____

_____

Countdown to Christmas

_____

_____

_____

_____

_____

_____

_____

_____

_____

_____

_____

_____

_____

_____

_____

_____

_____

_____

_____

_____

About the Author

Lisa Appelo is a writer and speaker who loves to proclaim God's faithfulness, especially in the hard. After becoming a sudden widow and single mom to 7, she and her children have seen firsthand that God is faithful and true. A former litigator, she's spent nearly 20 years home educating her children through high school and continues teaching her youngest two. She teaches a women's Sunday school class at First Baptist Church, Jacksonville and thrills to dig deep into God's Word. She loves to bake, to hang with her family and to run just enough to eat a daily dose of chocolate. She's a Florida girl and can be found at the following places:

www.LisaAppelo.com

INSTAGRAM: @LisaAppelo

FACEBOOK: /TrueandFaithful

TWITTER: @AppeloLisa

For encouragement and free Bible study resources, visit www.LisaAppelo.com

Countdown to Christmas

Countdown to Christmas

Countdown to Christmas

Made in the USA
Monee, IL
18 November 2021

82443219R00042